MY COMMUNITY

A DAY AT THE FIRE STATION

BY LORI MORTENSEN

ILLUSTRATED BY
JEFFREY THOMPSON

Consultant: Mark Klose, Deputy Chief
Bedford, New Hampshire Fire Department

CAPSTONE PRESS
a capstone imprint

WITHDRAWN

First Graphics are published by Capstone Press,
1710 Roe Crest Drive, North Mankato, Minnesota 56003.
www.capstonepub.com

Printed in the United States of America in Eau Claire, Wisconsin.

082013
007674R

Books published by Capstone Press are manufactured with paper containing at least 10 percent post-consumer waste.

Library of Congress Cataloging-in-Publication Data
Mortensen, Lori.
A day at the fire station / by Lori Mortensen ; illustrated by Jeffrey Thompson.
p. cm.—(First graphics. My community)
Includes bibliographical references and index.
Summary: "In graphic novel format, text and illustrations describe the daily activities of firefighters"—Provided by publisher.
ISBN 978-1-4296-4508-9 (library binding)
ISBN 978-1-4296-5612-2 (paperback)
1. Fire stations—Juvenile literature. 2. Fire fighters—Juvenile literature. I. Title. II. Series.
TH9148.M67 2011
628.9'25—dc22
2009051422

Editor: **Erika L. Shores**
Designer: **Alison Thiele**
Art Director: **Nathan Gassman**
Production Specialist: **Laura Manthe**

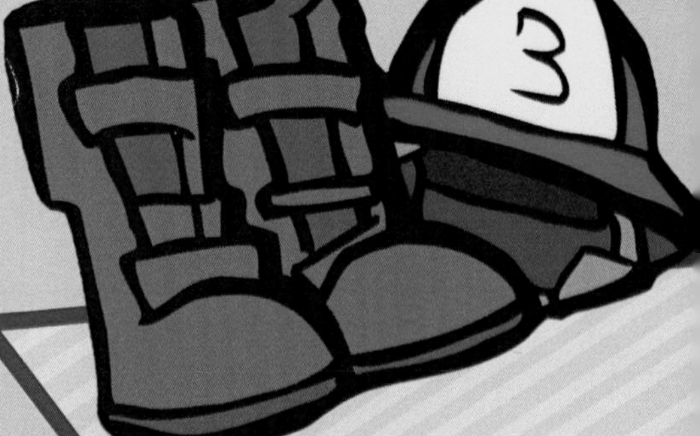
3

TABLE OF CONTENTS

FIRE HOUSE

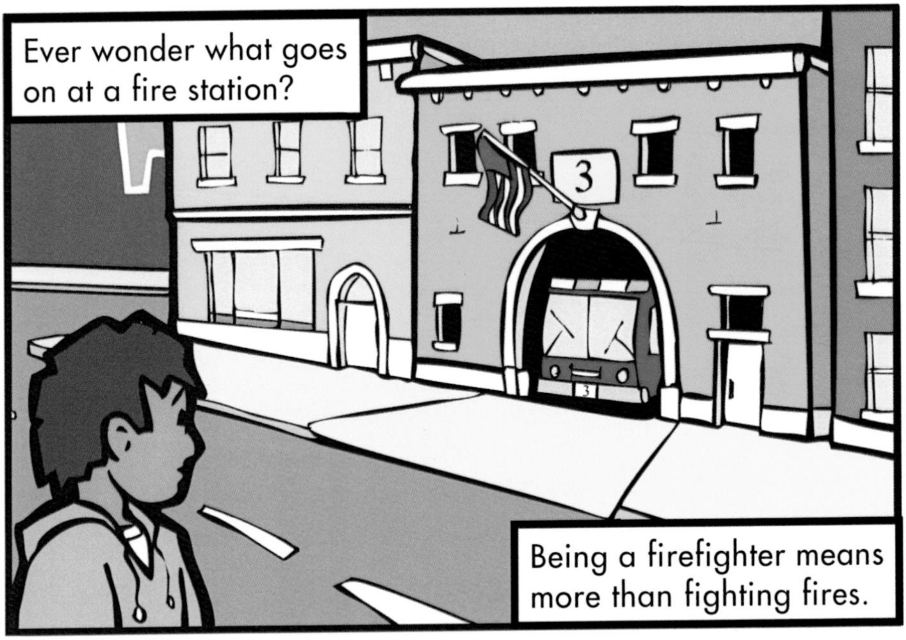
Ever wonder what goes on at a fire station?
Being a firefighter means more than fighting fires.

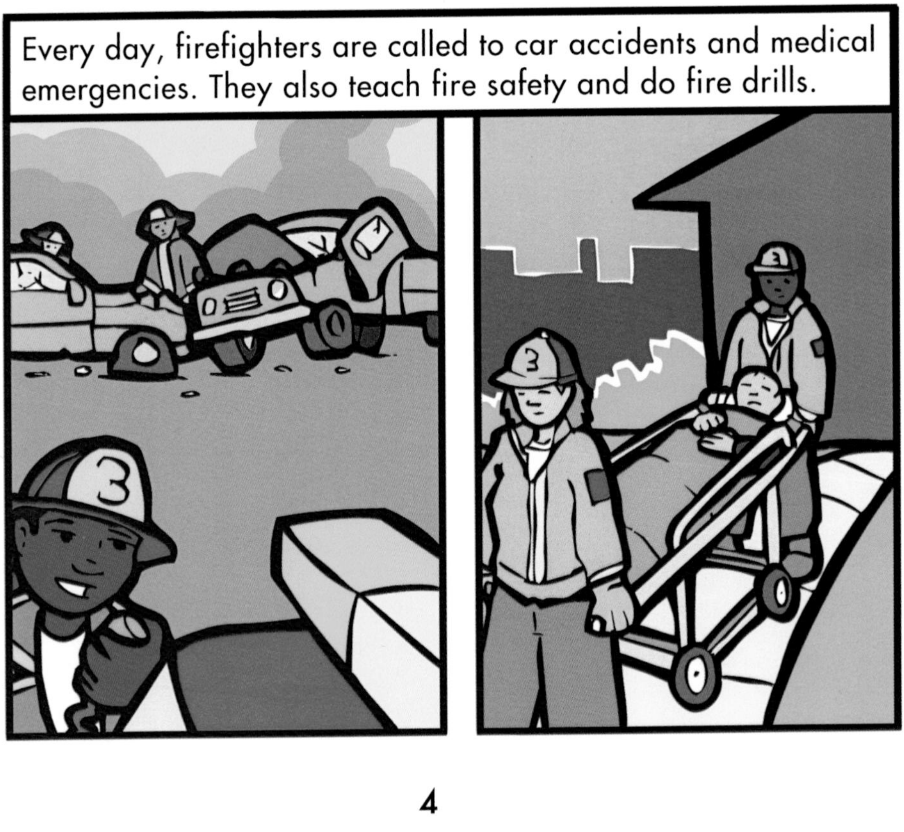
Every day, firefighters are called to car accidents and medical emergencies. They also teach fire safety and do fire drills.

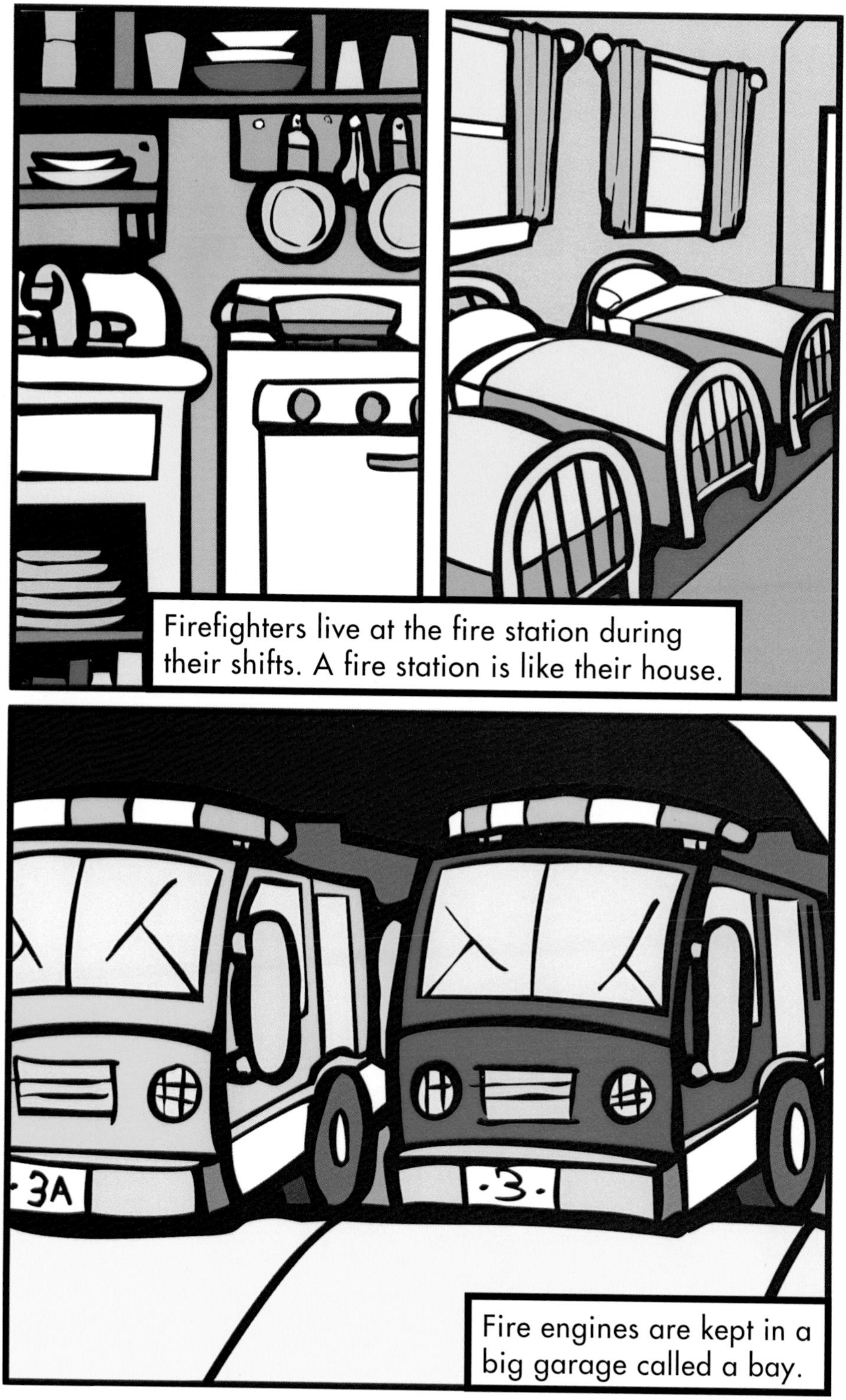
Firefighters live at the fire station during their shifts. A fire station is like their house.
3A
3
Fire engines are kept in a big garage called a bay.

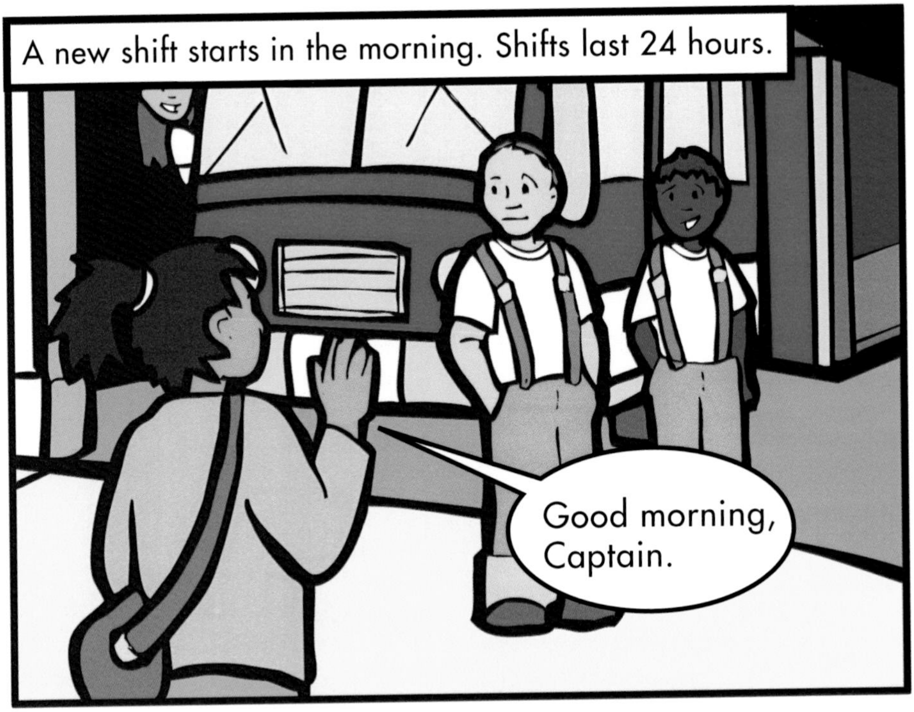
A new shift starts in the morning. Shifts last 24 hours.
Good morning, Captain.

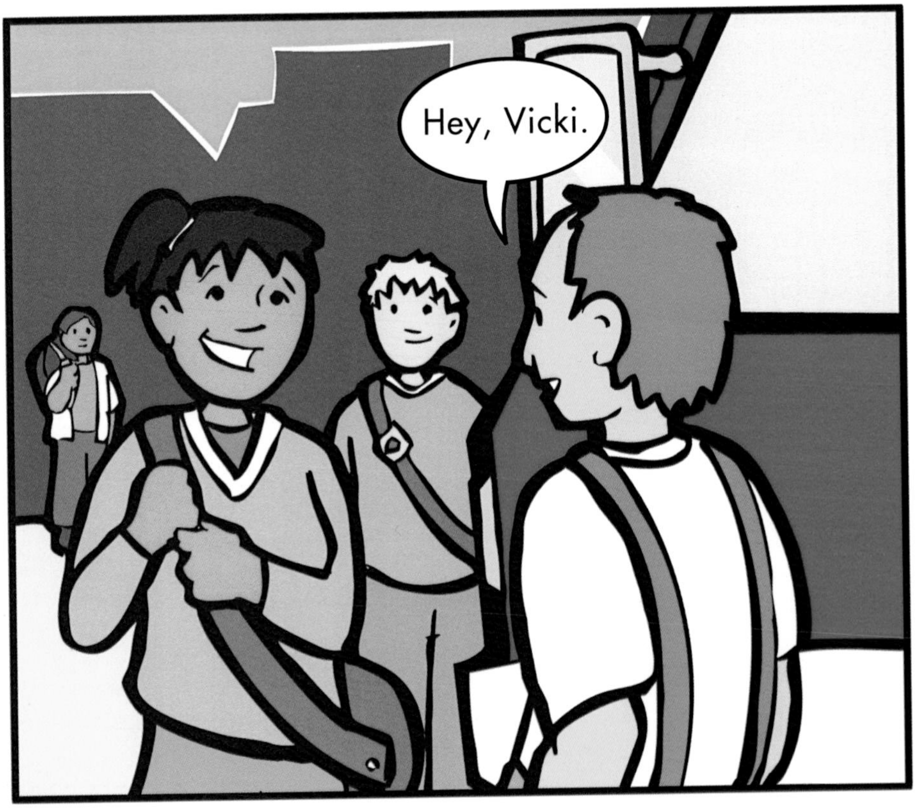
Hey, Vicki.

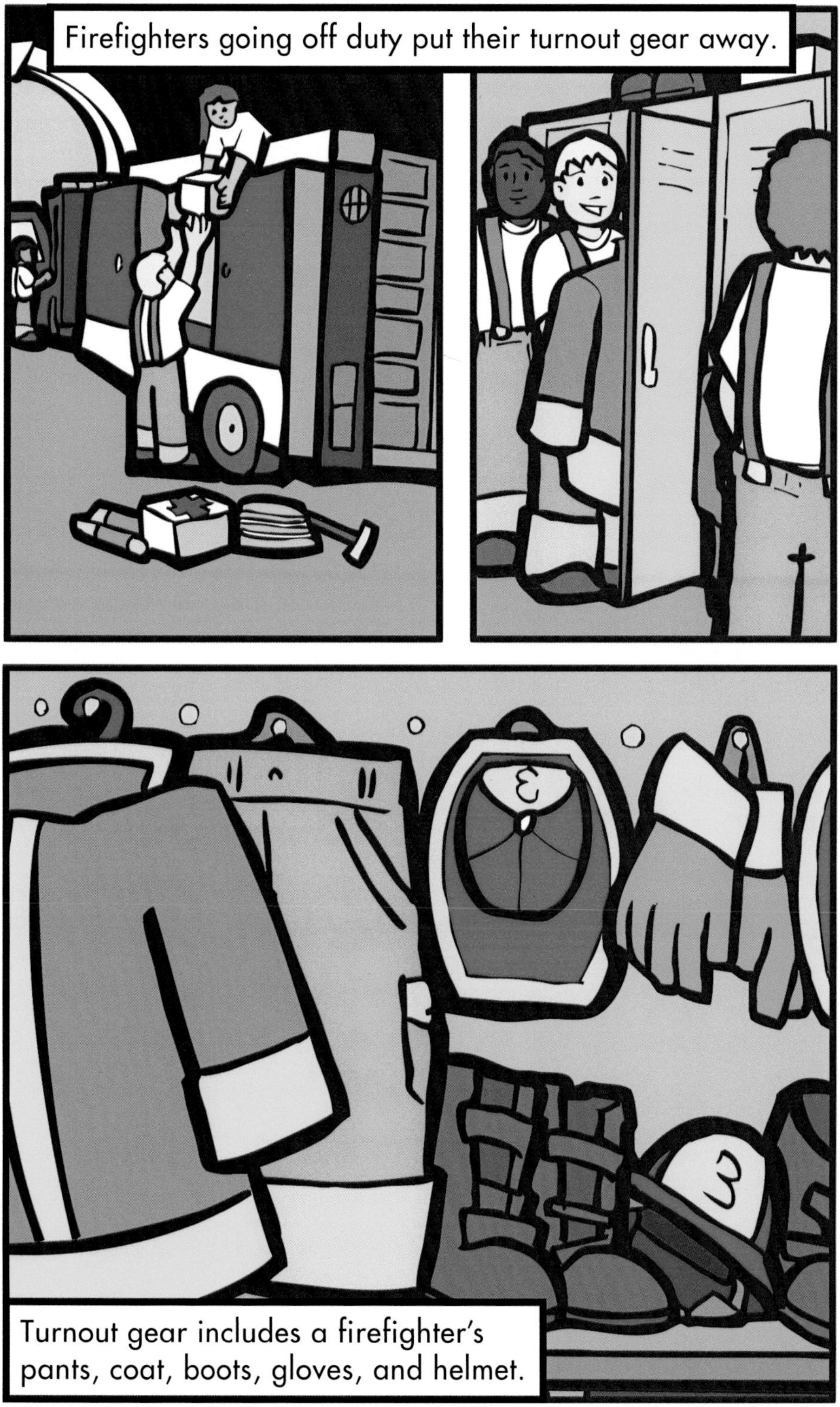
Firefighters going off duty put their turnout gear away.
Turnout gear includes a firefighter's pants, coat, boots, gloves, and helmet.

READY OR NOT?

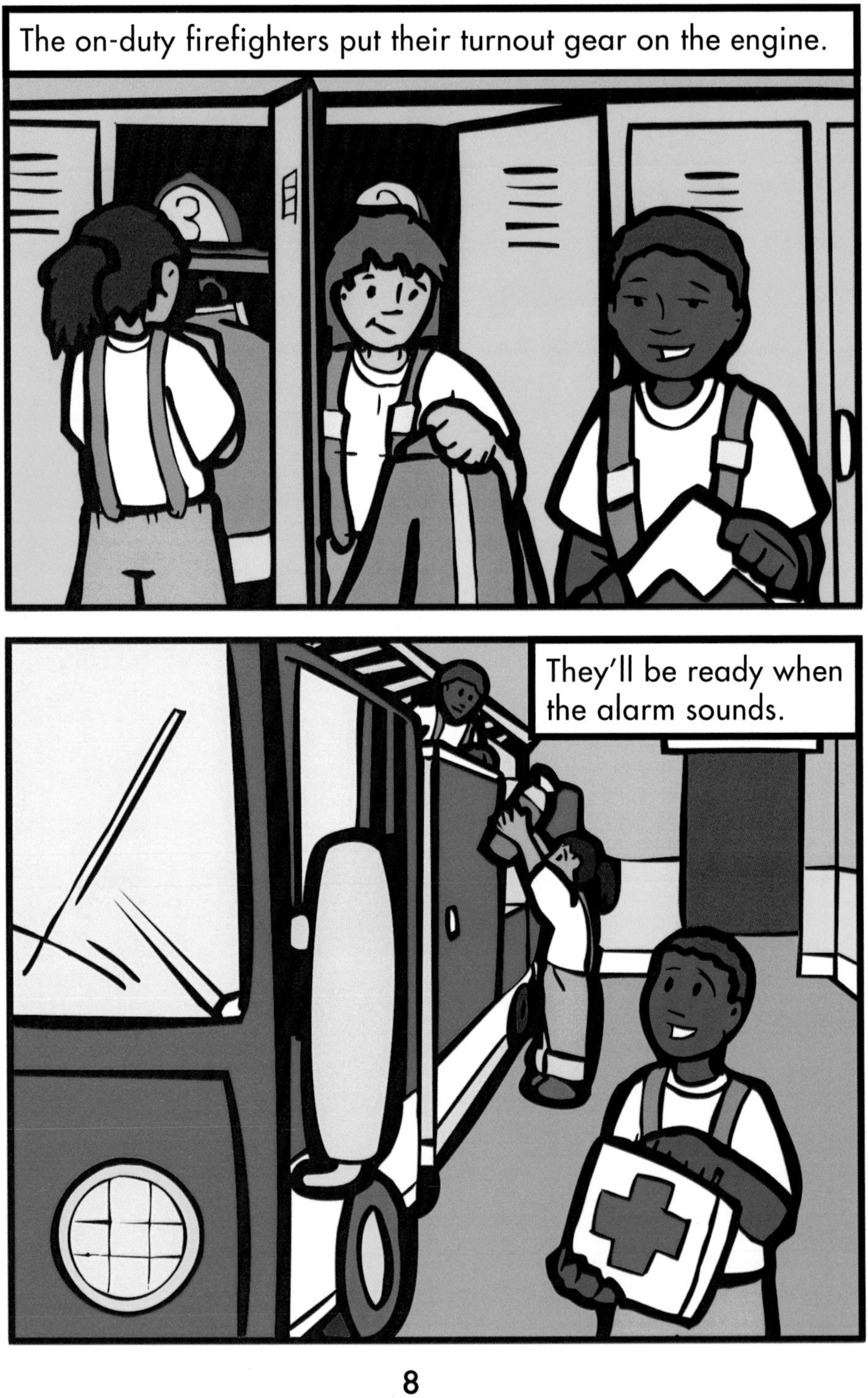
The on-duty firefighters put their turnout gear on the engine.
They'll be ready when the alarm sounds.

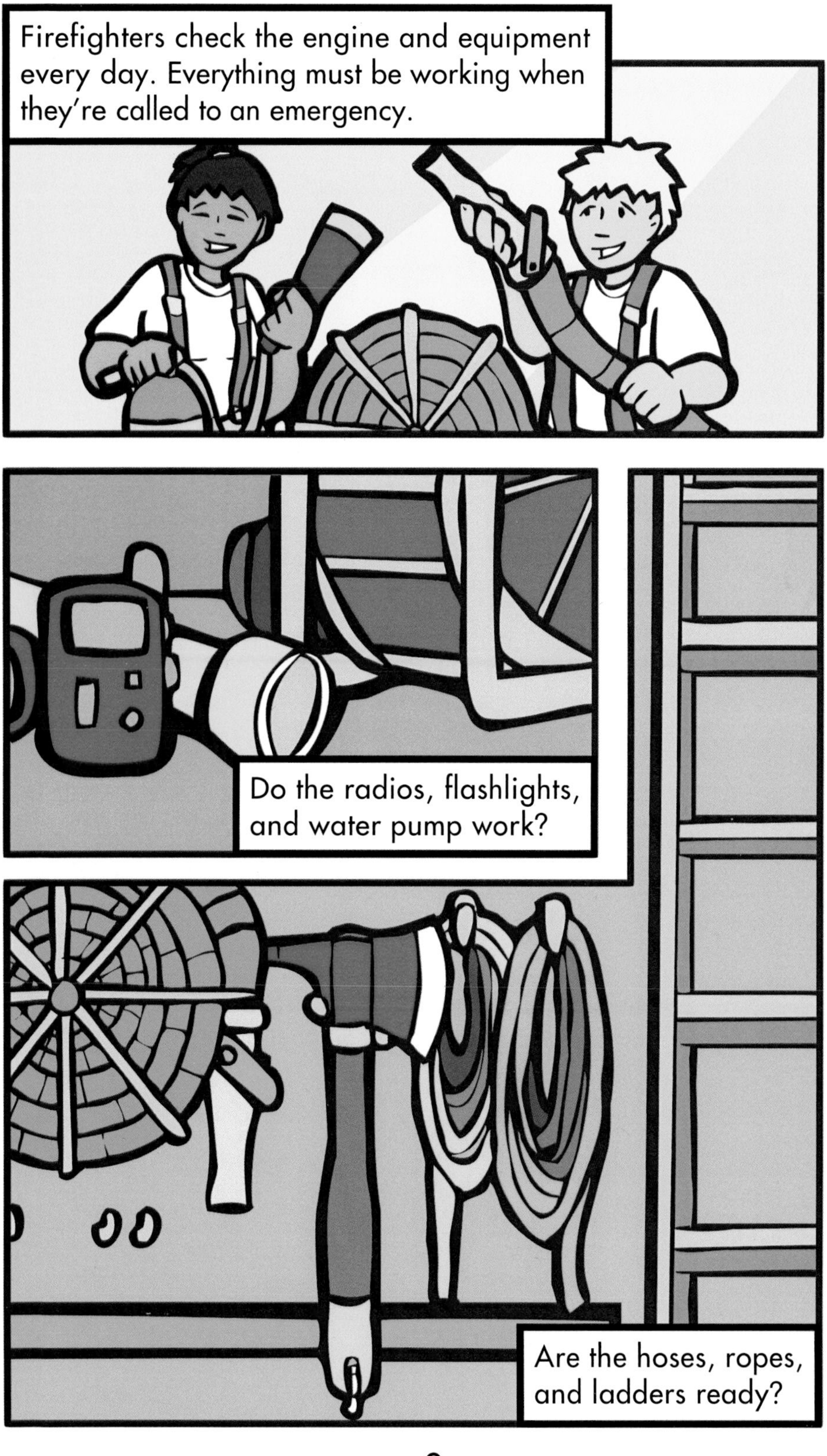
Firefighters check the engine and equipment every day. Everything must be working when they're called to an emergency.
Do the radios, flashlights, and water pump work?
Are the hoses, ropes, and ladders ready?

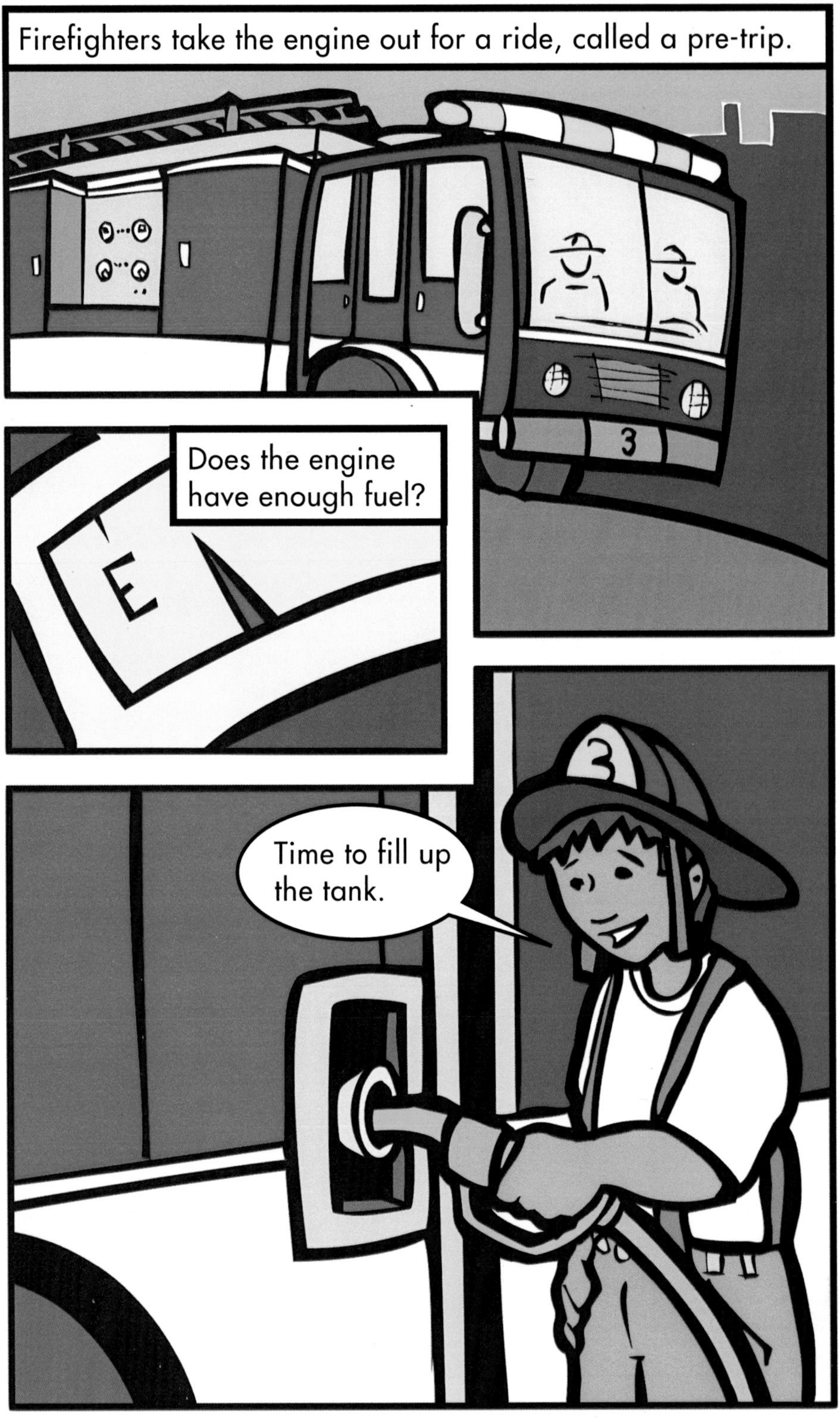
Firefighters take the engine out for a ride, called a pre-trip.
3
E
Does the engine have enough fuel?
3
Time to fill up the tank.

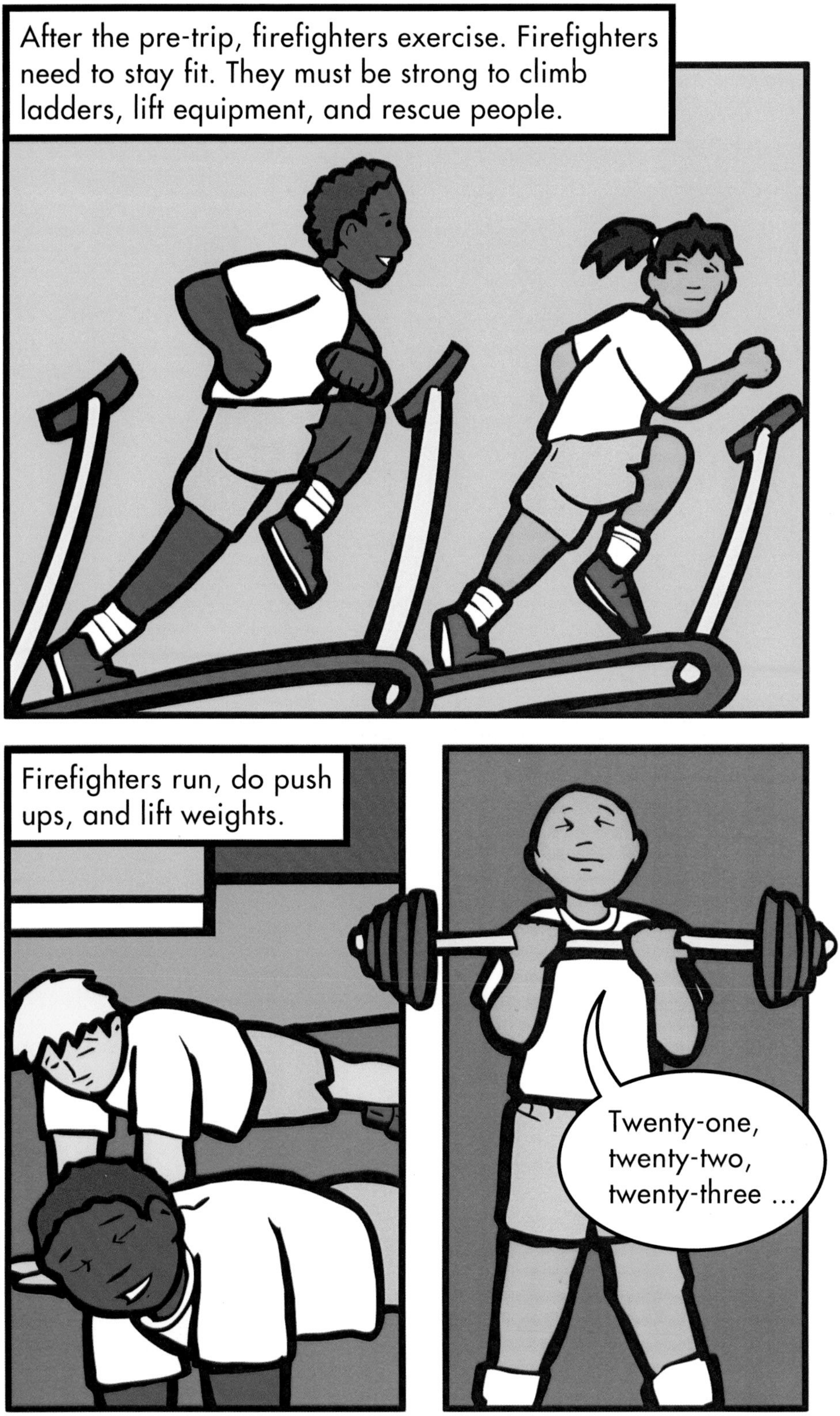
After the pre-trip, firefighters exercise. Firefighters need to stay fit. They must be strong to climb ladders, lift equipment, and rescue people.
Firefighters run, do push ups, and lift weights.
Twenty-one, twenty-two, twenty-three ...

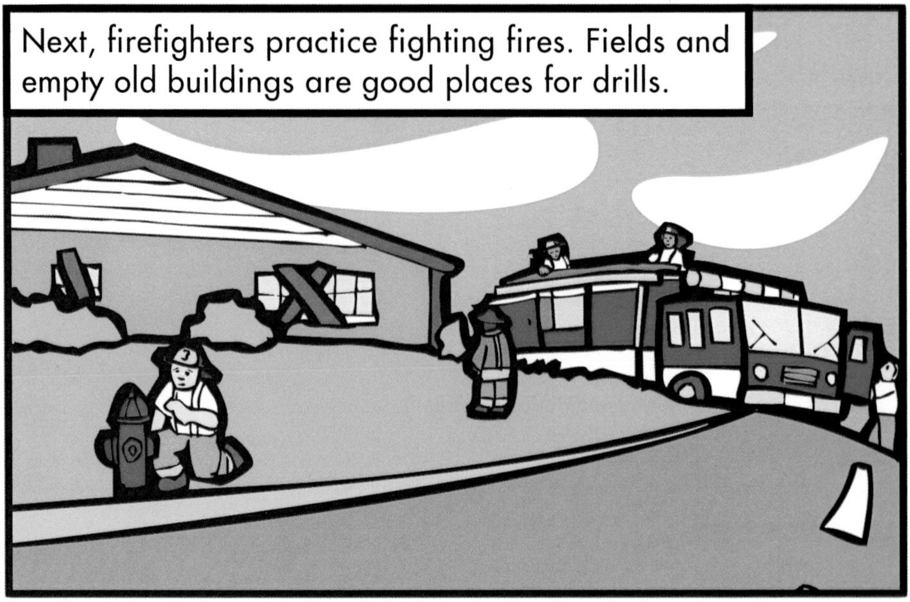
Next, firefighters practice fighting fires. Fields and empty old buildings are good places for drills.
3

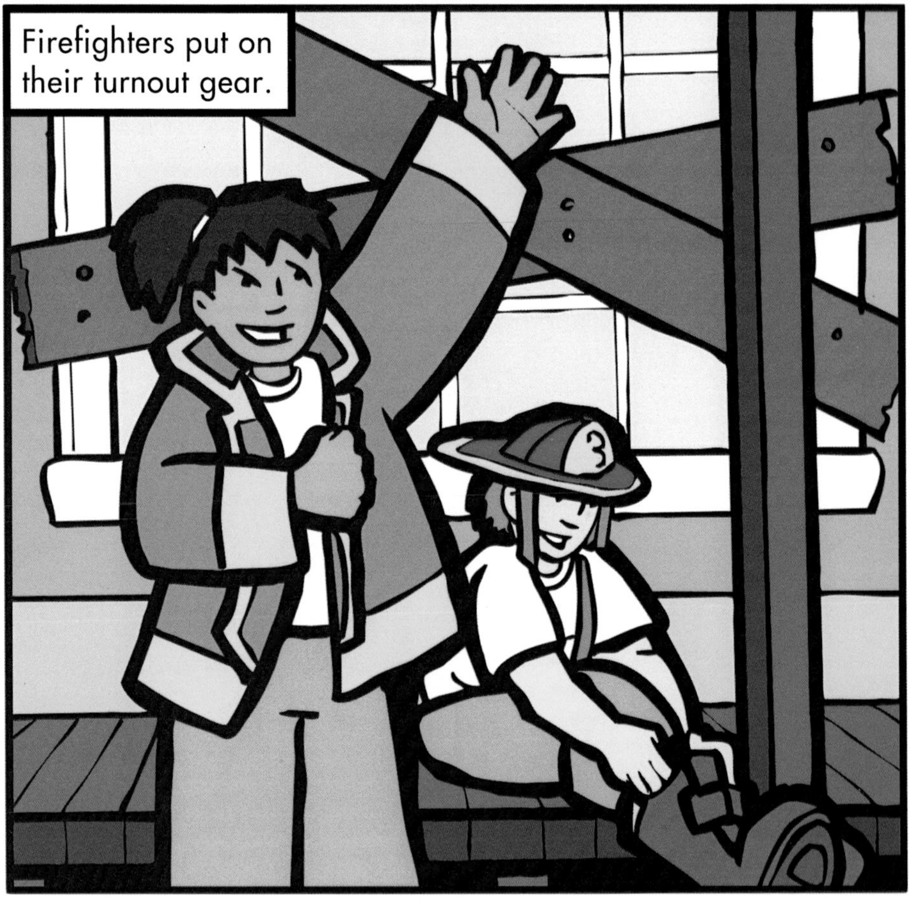
Firefighters put on their turnout gear.
3

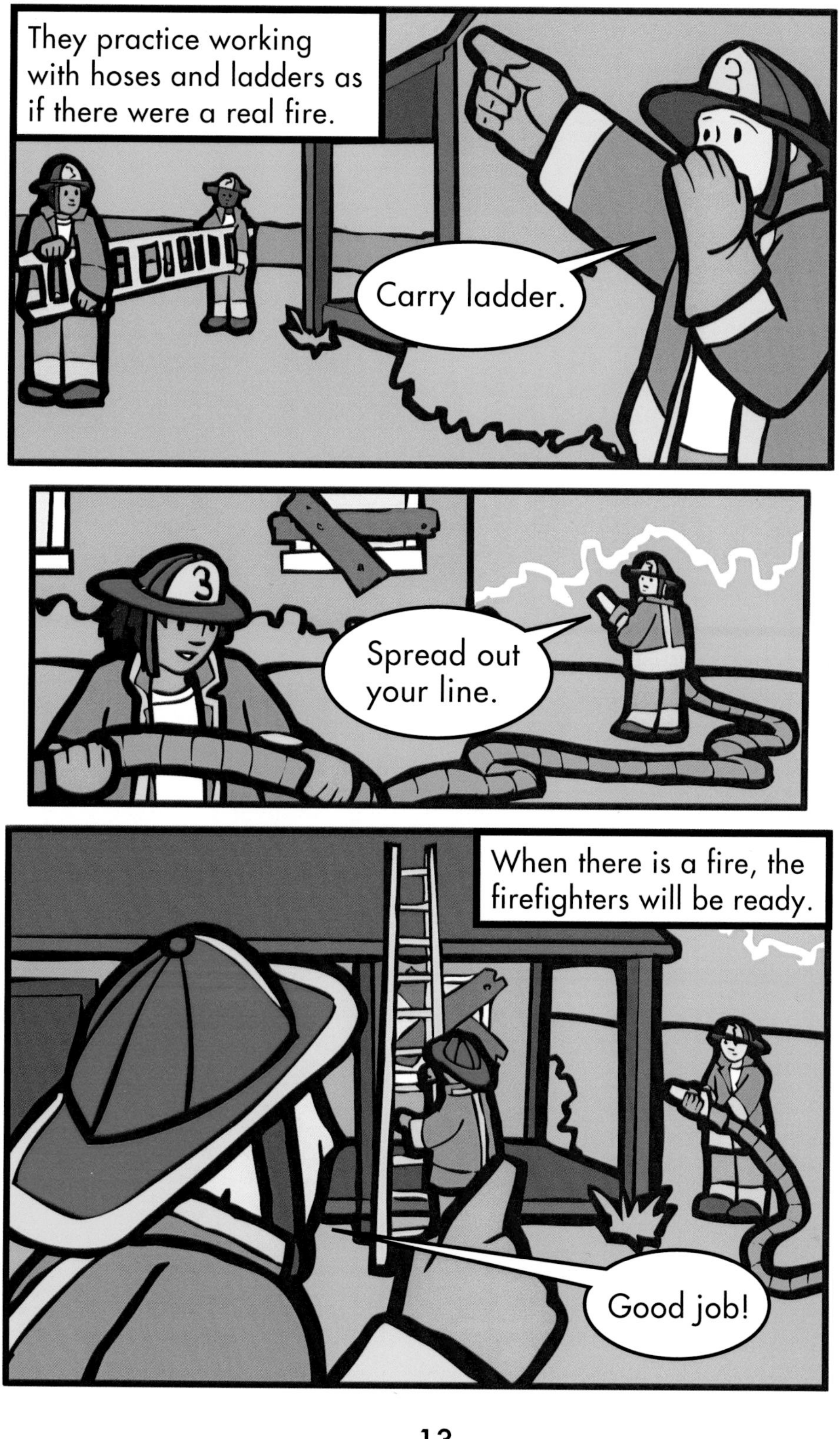
They practice working with hoses and ladders as if there were a real fire.
Carry ladder.
3
3
3
Spread out your line.
When there is a fire, the firefighters will be ready.
Good job!

ENGINE NUMBER 3

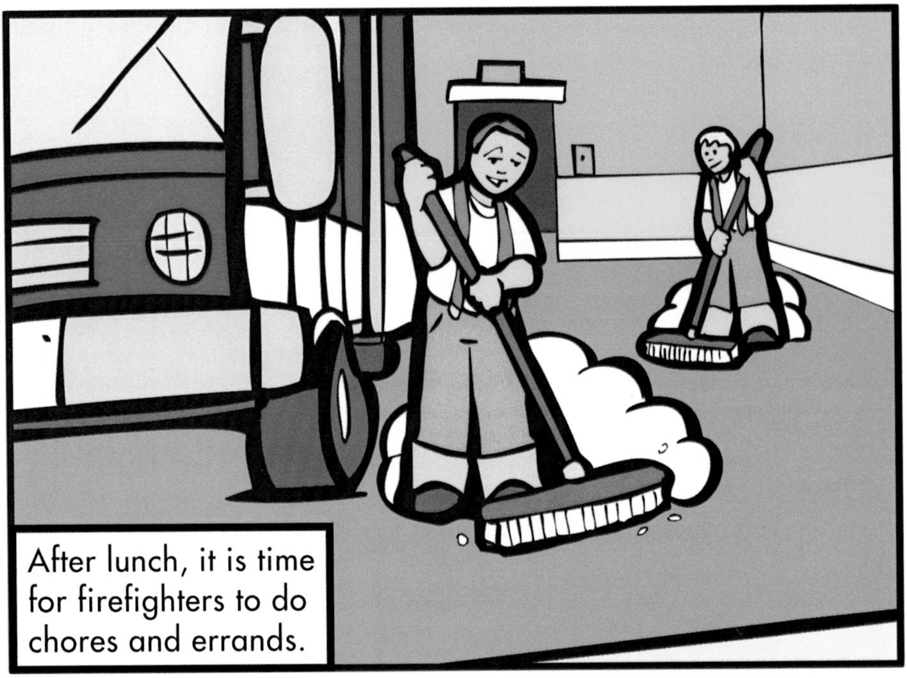
After lunch, it is time for firefighters to do chores and errands.

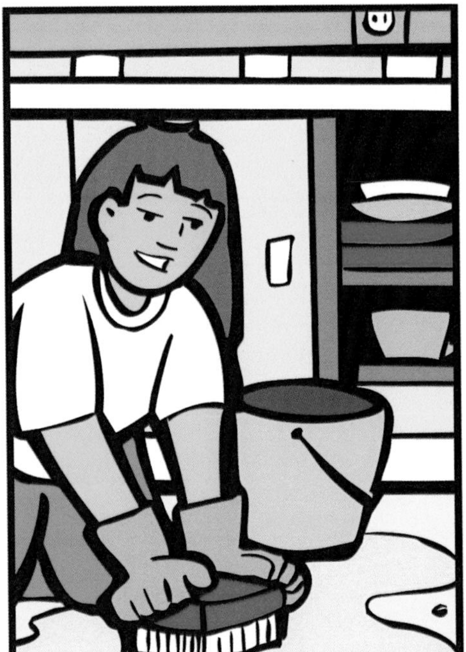

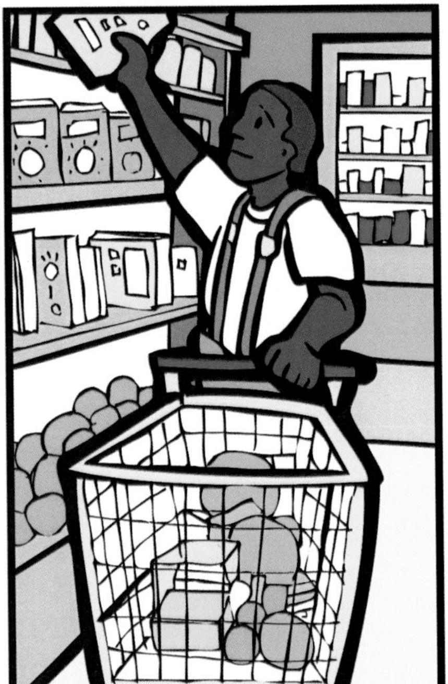

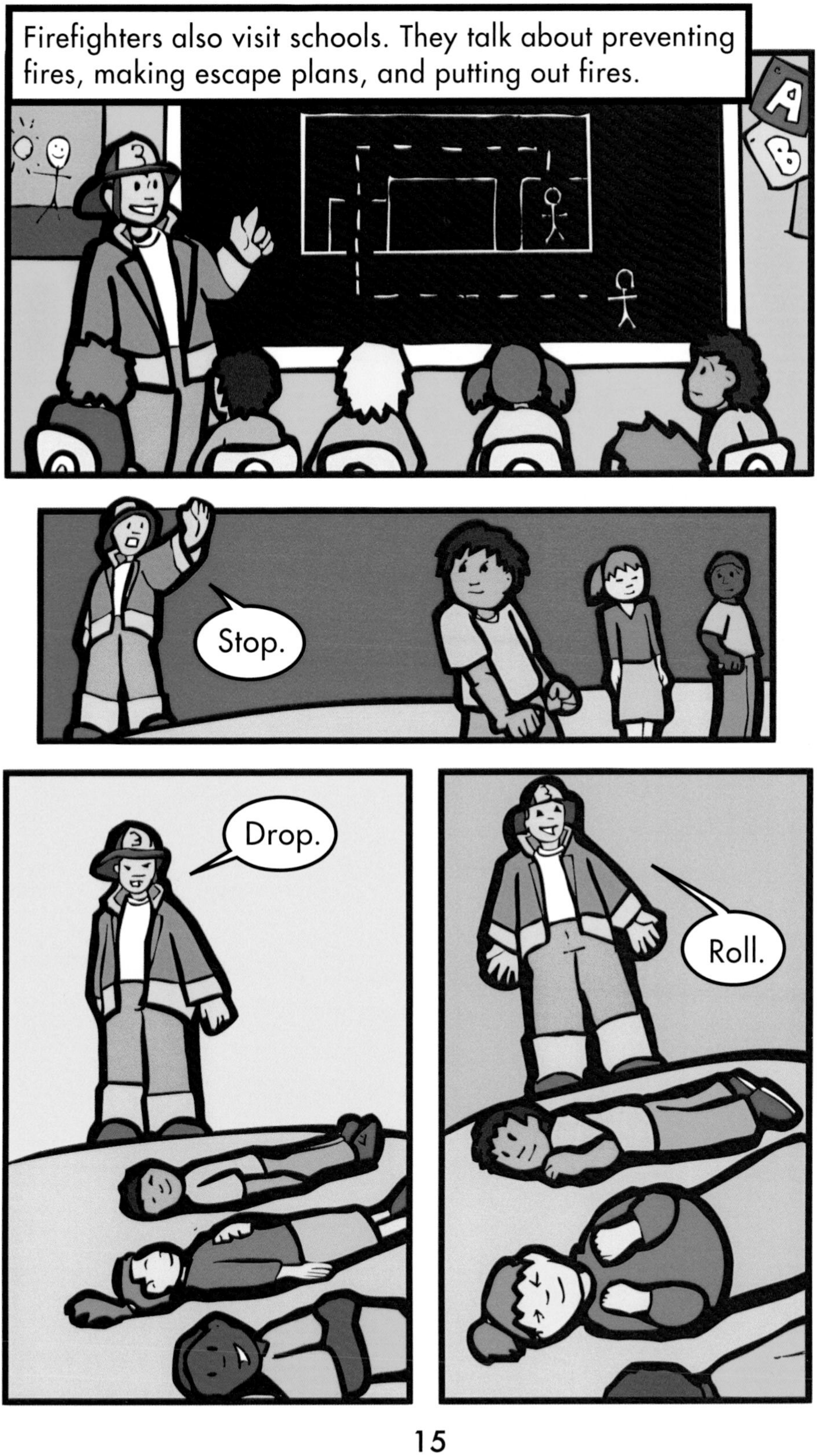
Firefighters also visit schools. They talk about preventing fires, making escape plans, and putting out fires.
Stop.
Drop.
Roll.

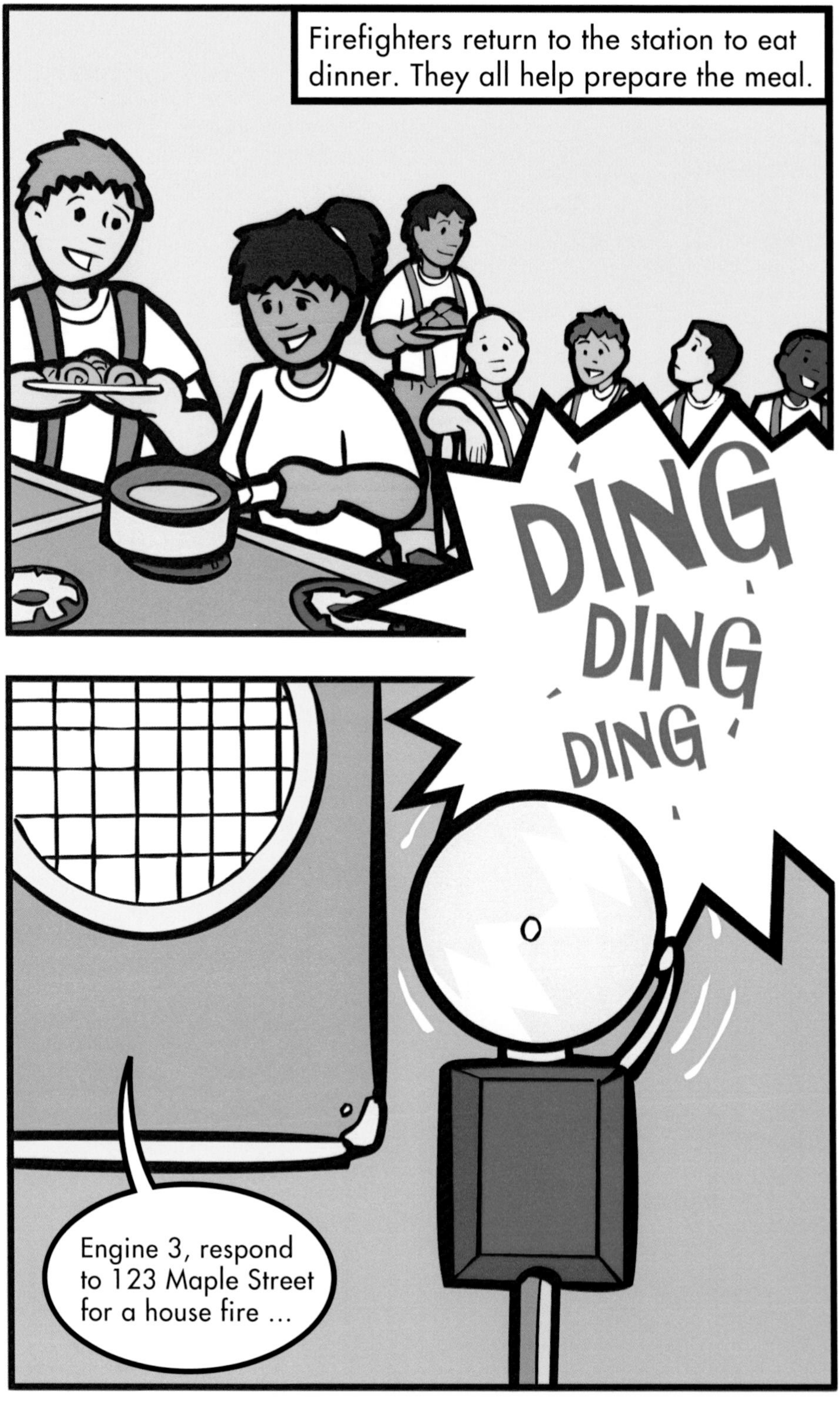
Firefighters return to the station to eat dinner. They all help prepare the meal.
DING
DING
DING
Engine 3, respond to 123 Maple Street for a house fire ...

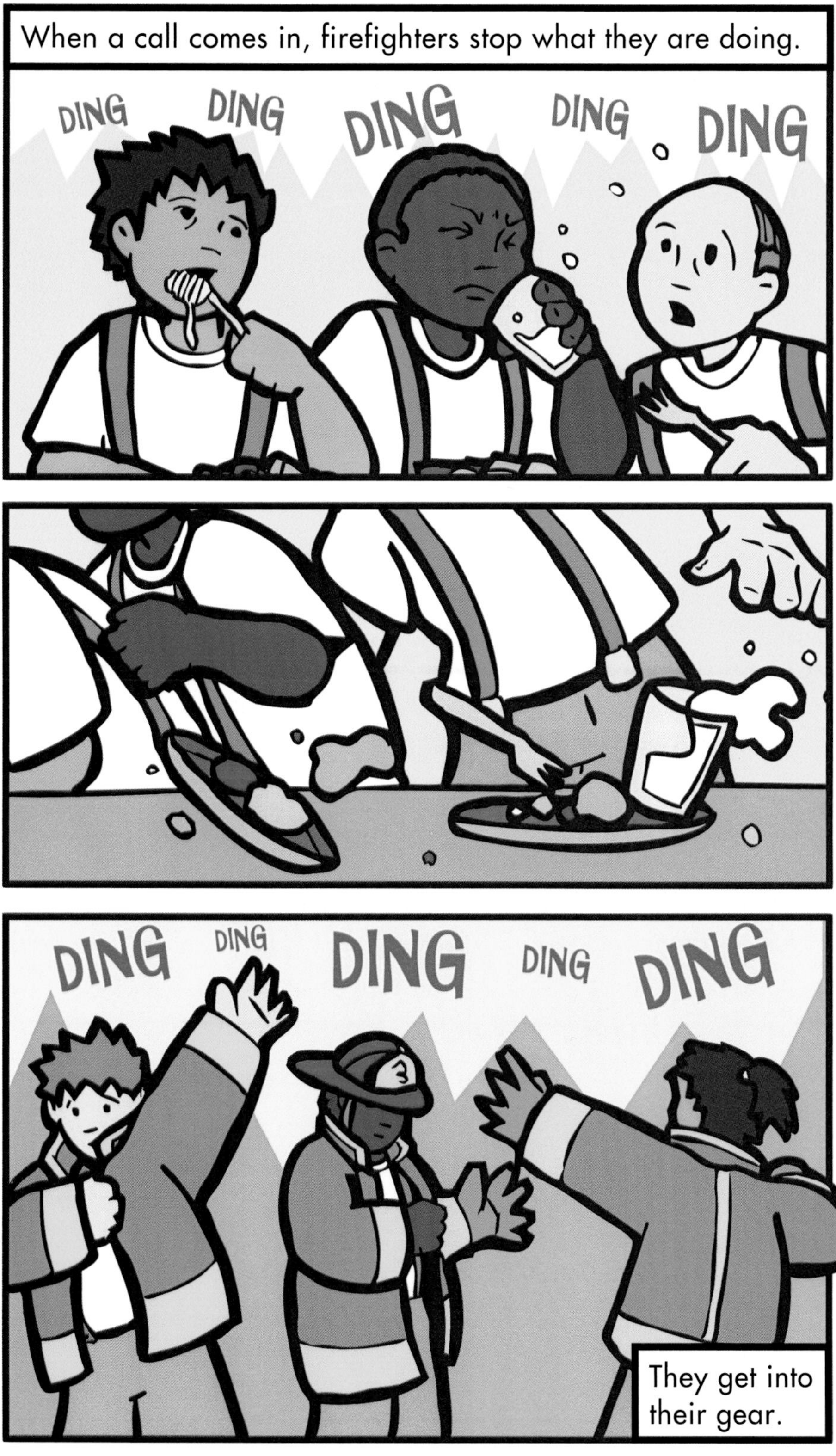
When a call comes in, firefighters stop what they are doing.
DING DING DING DING DING
DING DING DING DING DING
They get into their gear.

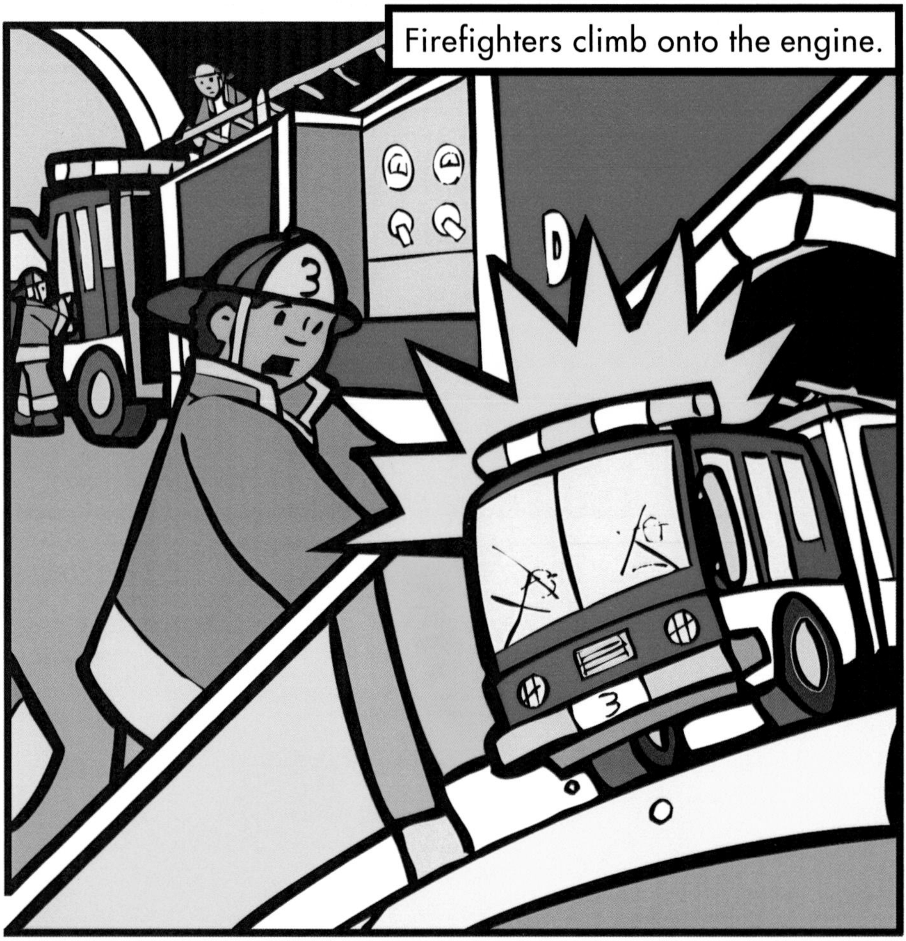
Firefighters climb onto the engine.
3
3

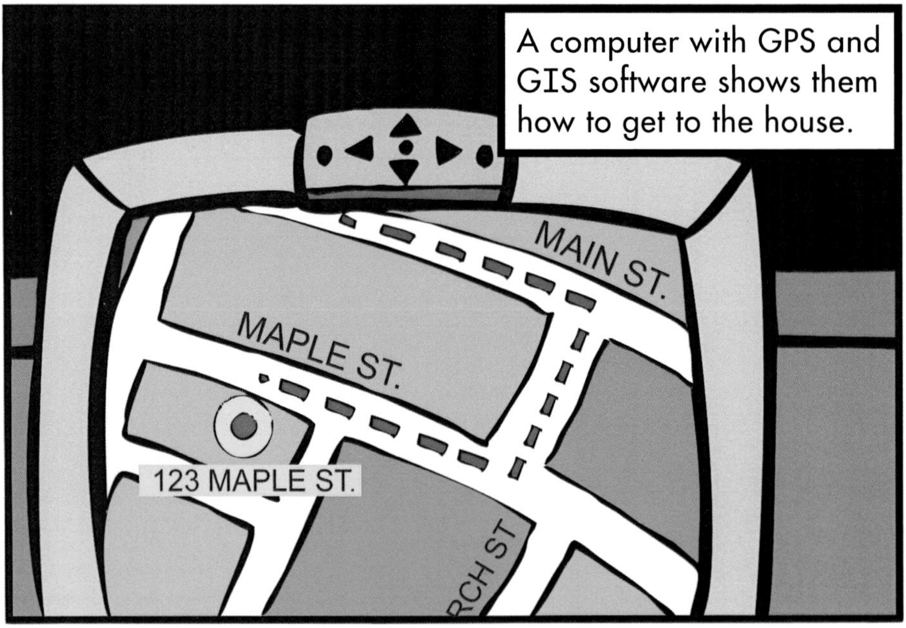
A computer with GPS and GIS software shows them how to get to the house.
MAIN ST.
MAPLE ST.
123 MAPLE ST.
RCH ST

When they arrive, the firefighters take out hoses and put up ladders.

Ready for water!

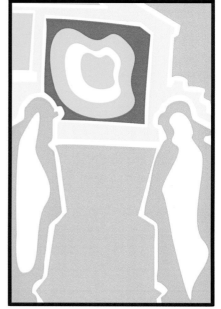

Water coming!

They use special cameras that show hidden hot spots. Hot spots are places that might still be on fire.

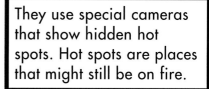

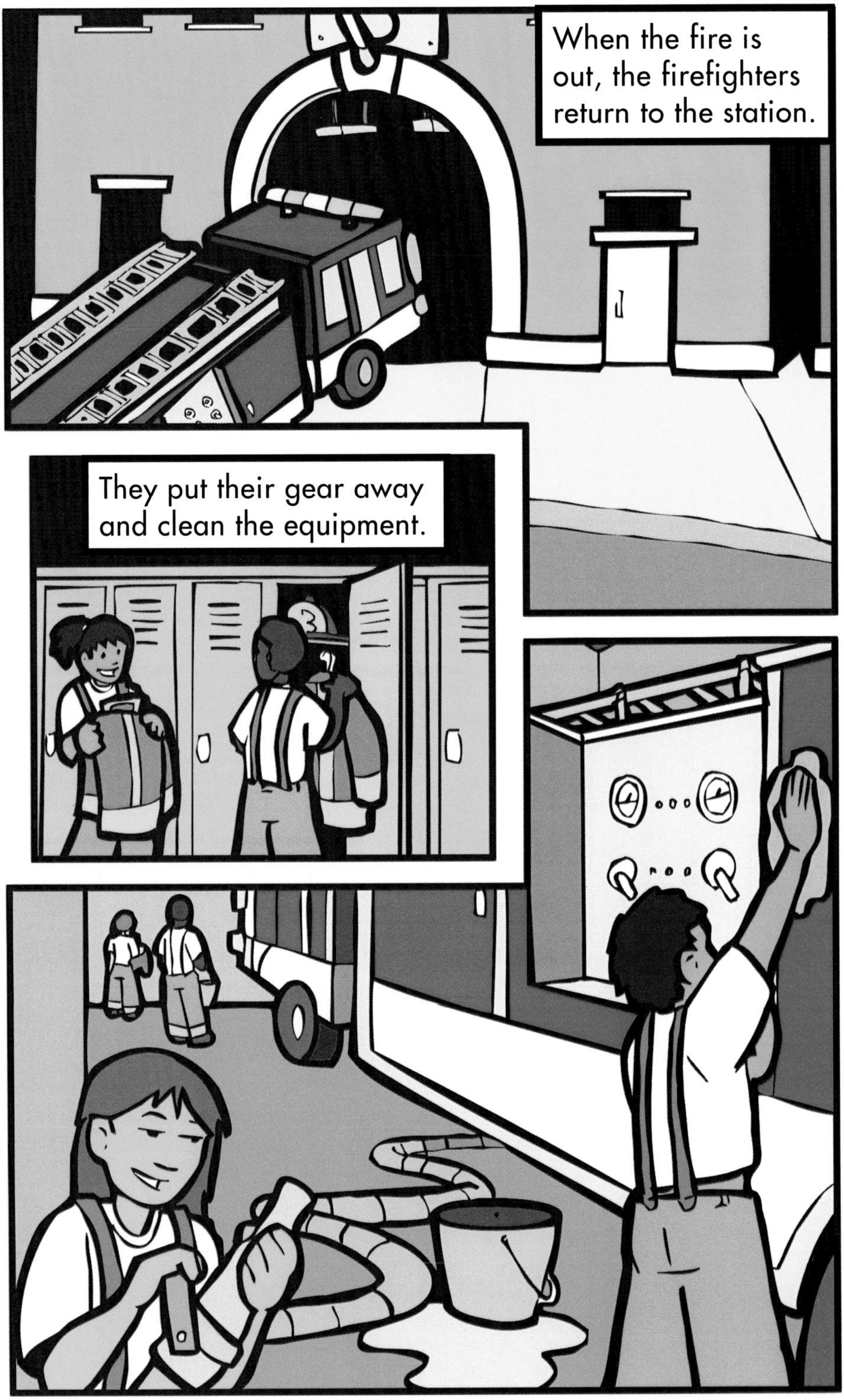
When the fire is out, the firefighters return to the station.
They put their gear away and clean the equipment.

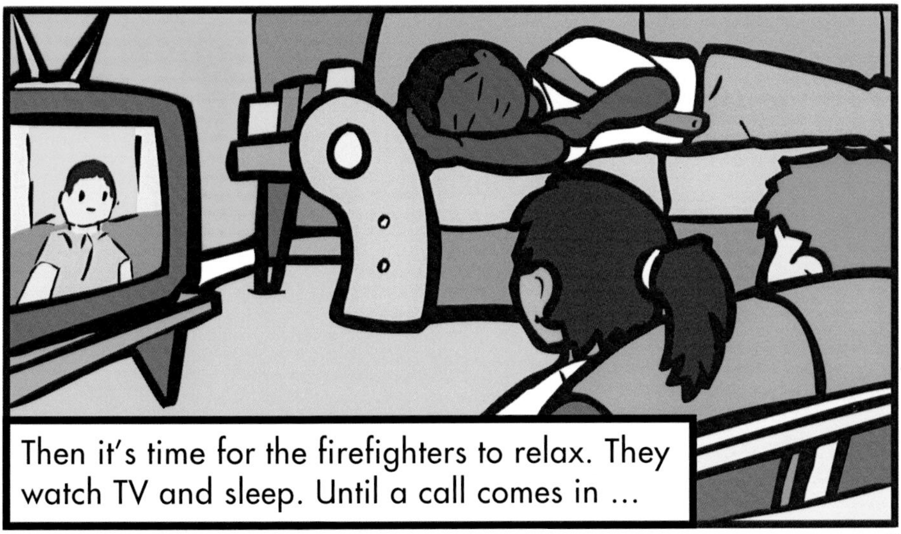
Then it's time for the firefighters to relax. They watch TV and sleep. Until a call comes in ...

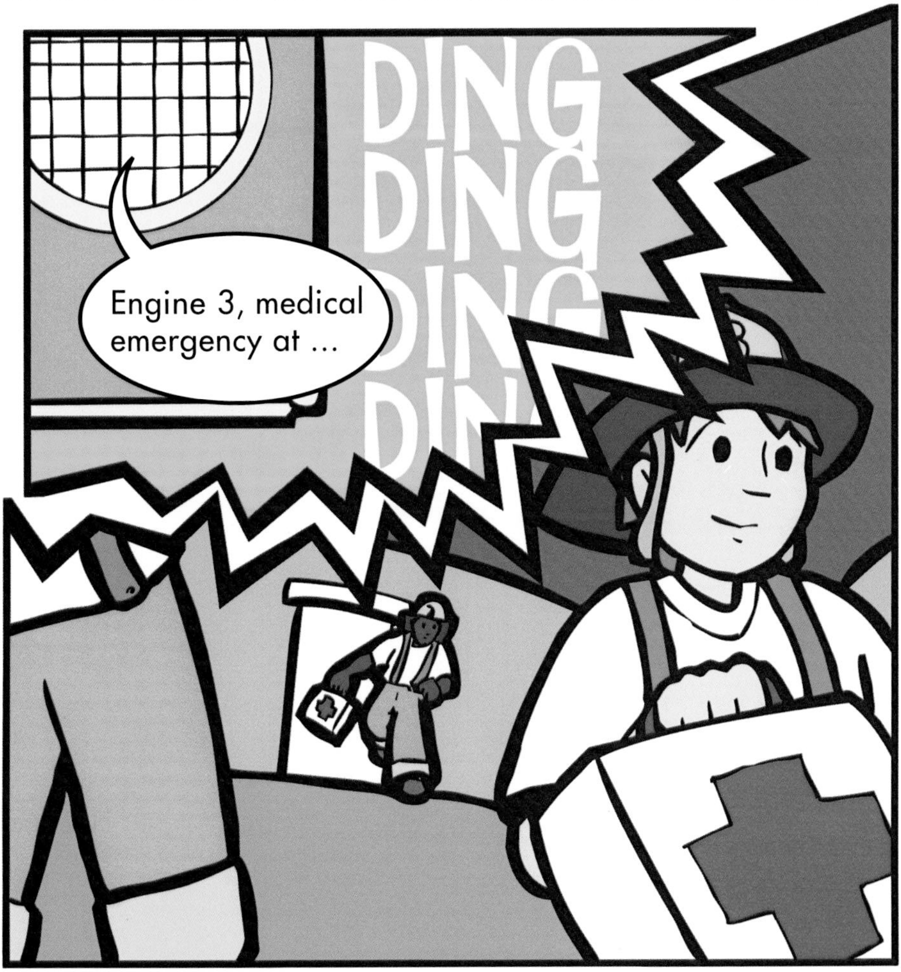
DING
DING
Engine 3, medical emergency at ...

GLOSSARY

bay—the area of a fire station that holds fire engines and other equipment

drill—an exercise repeated over and over to practice a skill

emergency—a sudden and dangerous situation that must be handled quickly

engine—a firefighting vehicle that pumps water

GIS—a system for geography that gives information about physical features such buildings, land, water, and roads; GIS stands for geographic information system

GPS—an electronic tool used to find the location of a person or object anywhere on Earth; GPS stands for global positioning system

pre-trip—a trip taken by firefighters in the engine to decide if it's ready for an emergency

shift—the period of time a firefighter is on duty

turnout gear—the special clothes a firefighter wears when fighting fires

READ MORE

Armentrout, David and Patricia. *The Fire Department.* Our Community. Vero Beach, Fla.: Rourke Publishing, 2009.

Schuh, Mari. *Fire Stations in Action.* Fighting Fire. Mankato, Minn.: Capstone Press, 2009.

Spilsbury, Louise. *At a Fire Station.* Technology at Work. Chicago: Raintree, 2009.

INTERNET SITES

FactHound offers a safe, fun way to find Internet sites related to this book. All of the sites on FactHound have been researched by our staff.

Here's all you do:

Visit *www.facthound.com*

FactHound will fetch the best sites for you!

INDEX

MY COMMUNITY

TITLES IN THIS SET:

A DAY AT THE
FIRE STATION

GOING TO THE
DENTIST

A VISIT TO THE
VET

WORKING ON THE
FARM